"This book connects the dots for you every level of management. Pete brir and motivation to the surface. Stop \ find the magic of HOW?"

—JEFF PETERSON | Co-Founder/CEO, Geneva Supply

"Successful organizations understand the value of adding Disney magic to all areas of their company. Pete Blank shows you multiple ways you can add magic to improve in the areas of leadership, cast experience, guest service, and business processes."

—LEE COCKERELL | Executive VP (retired), Walt Disney World Resort
Author of *Creating Magic*, *The Customer Rules*, *Time Management Magic*, and *Career Magic*

"Pete Blank helped us add Disney magic to our community college. This book shares multiple ways that you can move your college, company, or non-profit organization from average to excellent...with just a little bit of Disney magic!"

—DR. RUSS ROTHAMER | Executive Vice President, Aims Community College

"Pete Blank shares some practical yet insightful tips to develop leaders within any organization. It all begins with YOU."

—OPAL MAULDIN-JONES | ICMA CM, City Manager

# 55 Ways
## to Add Disney Magic to Your Organization

Pete Blank

No part of this book may be reproduced in any form or by any electronic or mechanical means including, but not limited to, printing, photocopying, audio or video recording, electronic replication, information storage and retrieval systems, and internet distribution without permission in writing from the author. The only exception is by a reviewer, who may quote short excerpts in a review. All international copyright laws apply.

All trademarks, service marks, product names and company names are assumed to be the property of their respective owners and are used only for reference. There is no implied endorsement by those entities. Likewise, the fact that an organization or website is referenced in this work as a potential source of further information does not mean that the author or the publisher endorses, has confirmed, or warrants the information provided in this book or in those references.

Printed in the United States of America

Copyright © 2020 Pete Blank
All rights reserved.
Library of Congress Control Number: 2020907581
ISBN-10: 978-1-7346565-0-3

# Dedication

To Sherri – thank you for supporting me, loving me, and encouraging me.

To Madison and Logan - thank you for loving Disney as much as I do.

To Eric Atkins - thanks for the brilliant idea.

To Brian Vagi and Debi Immel - thank you for your insight and editing skills

To Kendra Cagle - thank you for your awesome typesetting.

To my friends in the Disney Circle - thank you for being a significant part of an amazing 13 years of my life. You all made the magic for me every day.

To Jeff and Lorren - thank you for allowing me the capacity to share my passion for Disney with others.

To God – thank you for your Son, Jesus Christ.

# Receive More Tips from Pete Blank

## Keynotes and Workshops
Pete provides keynote speeches and workshops to companies and organizations around the United States. All his topics can be viewed on his website. You can contact him at **peteblank@peteblank.com** or **407-376-8384**.

## Pete's Points
**VIDEO:** Pete has recorded over one hundred video lessons on leadership, customer service, business strategy, and professional development. Find out more at **www.peteblank.com**.

**AUDIO:** Pete hosts one of the longest continuous running Alexa Flash Briefings! These daily audio lessons help managers, leaders, and individual contributors add value to their organizations. You can subscribe to these daily points by enabling the Pete's Points Alexa Skill on your Amazon Alexa device, or visit his website at **www.peteblank.com/alexa-daily-flashbriefs** to subscribe on Apple Podcasts, Google Play, iHeart Radio, Spotify, Pandora, and anywhere podcasts are streaming.

## Social Media
Pete would love to connect with you on social media.
- **f** @petespoints
- **🐦** @peteblank
- **in** @peteblank

## Other Books by Pete
Pete's first book, *Employee Engagement: Lessons from the Mouse House* is available on www.amazon.com.

## For Bulk Orders
Group Discounts are available for book orders of 10 or more. Please email Pete directly at **peteblank@peteblank.com** for information.

# Prologue / Forward

Most people who know me know that I am passionate about all things Disney. My goal of working for this organization was fulfilled when I spent 13 years working at The Walt Disney World Resort. From an attractions host at The Great Movie Ride to a Bell Services Manager at Port Orleans Resort...from an Educational Consultant for the Disney College Program to a Segment Learning Manager at Disney University, I loved every minute of my Disney experience.

I am the Training and Organizational Development manager for the Personnel Board of Jefferson County in Birmingham, Alabama. I take many of my Disney learnings on employee engagement, the Disney "show", and customer service and apply them to civil service in Alabama.

I continue to travel the country sharing leadership lessons and business strategies with organizations in the for-profit, non-profit, and educational fields, and I am so blessed to be able to do what I do.

## A couple of thoughts about this book:

- As a general rule, when I use the term "Disney," I am talking about the Disney Parks and Resorts segment. As the company has expanded, some of these principles may not apply to other divisions such as television and film, corporate merchandising, feature animation, and so on. If I have a story or mention Walt Disney (the man), I will use his full name.

- "Onstage" and "backstage" are terms used by Disney to describe different roles. Onstage refers to Cast Members who work directly with guests, while backstage Cast Members work in areas that may not have direct contact with the guests.

- Why 55 tips? Why not 50, or 75, or 100? Disneyland Theme Park opened July 17, **1955**. Without that magical summer of '55, I would never have had my Disney experience, and this book would not be in your hands right now.

This tip book can be used in multiple ways. If you are a manager, you can bring one tip to your weekly staff meetings, read the chapter, and talk about the **ACTION ITEMS** as a team. If you are an individual contributor, you can apply some of these lessons to yourself, your co-workers, or your teammates.

Most importantly, I hope you use this book as a resource to become better in both your personal and professional lives. Thanks for reading, and I hope I can meet you in person one day.

## Now go make magic in your organization

—Pete

# Table of Contents

## The Magic of Leadership

*Want to improve your leadership skills? Want to apply some Disney leadership strategies to assist you on your personal journey? Are you a CEO, manager, or aspiring supervisor? Then these chapters are for you!*

1. Make Employee Development a Top Priority
2. Treat your Direct Reports as Valuable Assets
3. Provide Regular One-on-One Meetings with your Direct Reports
4. Harness the Power of Cross-Utilization
5. Be Ready and Able to "Jump In" When Needed
6. Fix all Mistakes with a "Guest First" Attitude
7. Learn and live the concept of "Business Savvy"
8. Act Like a Leader at all Times
9. Share your Expectations with your Direct Reports within the First Week
10. Have Awareness Beyond your own Department
11. Be a Leadership R.O.L.E. Model
12. Make Employee Recognition a Top Priority
13. Place the Right Employees into the Right Jobs for the Right Reasons
14. Communicate the Overall Purpose of Every Role
15. Hire for Attitude and Train for Skill
16. Promote From Within Whenever Possible

## The Magic of the Employees

*Do you want to be the best employee you can be? Whether you are a manager, supervisor, or individual contributor, these chapters will help you add magic to your everyday work.*

| | |
|---|---|
| 17. | Learn to Love your Job |
| 18. | Learn to Love your Organization |
| 19. | Learn to Love your Boss |
| 20. | Learn to Love your Squad |
| 21. | Utilize Intrinsic Motivation over Insurmountable Money |
| 22. | Create a Successful Recognition Program |
| 23. | Look for a Right-Fit Role |
| 24. | Take Advantage of Professional Development Opportunities |
| 25. | Allow Creativity and Innovation to Flourish |
| 26. | Showcase the Employee Success Stories |
| 27. | Create a Fun Work Environment |
| 28. | Choose to be Engaged instead of Disengaged |

## The Magic of the Customer Experience

*Do you want your customer service to be amazing? Do you have a passion for creating a customer service experience as magical as Disney? Then this is the section for you.*

| | |
|---|---|
| 29. | Make Eye Contact with your Guests |
| 30. | Provide a Welcoming Greeting |
| 31. | Approach and Be Approachable |
| 32. | Offer Service Recovery Quickly |
| 33. | Exhibit Appropriate Body Language |

| | |
|---|---|
| 34. | Keep Backstage Stuff Backstage |
| 35. | Thank Every Guest Every Time |
| 36. | Be a Guest in your own Organization |
| 37. | Create a Sense of Anticipation |
| 38. | Deliver an Amazing Welcome |
| 39. | Produce a Powerful, Unforgettable Experience |
| 40. | Provide a Proper Guest Farewell |
| 41. | Allow Guests to Savor the Experience |
| 42. | Generate a Consistent Guest Experience |
| 43. | Create Emotional and Relational Connections |
| 44. | Add Creativity to your Customer Service |

## The Magic of Successful Business Processes

*Do you want your company to be the best? Do you have a passion for creating a successful organization? This section is for you. These chapters are designed for the CEO, management, and leadership teams, but there are plenty of Disney tips here that anyone at any level can add to their workplace.*

| | |
|---|---|
| 45. | Share the Heritage and Traditions of your Organization |
| 46. | Use Leadership Development for Succession Planning |
| 47. | Live your Vision/Mission/Values every day |
| 48. | Research your Competition |
| 49. | Always put Company over Department |
| 50. | Showcase your Organization in New and Unusual Ways |
| 51. | Embrace the Concept of Synergy |
| 52. | Allow for a Culture of Creative Risk-Taking |
| 53. | Provide Multiple "Streams of Purpose" for all Employees |
| 54. | Look for Ways to Enhance the Process |
| 55. | Remember that an Employee's First Day is their Most Important Day |

# Section One

# The Magic of Leadership

*Want to improve your leadership skills?*
*Want to apply some Disney leadership strategies*
*to assist you on your personal journey?*
*Are you a CEO, manager, or aspiring supervisor?*

*Then these chapters are for you!*

# 1.
## Make Employee Development a Top Priority

When it comes to developing leaders, it is imperative that organizations provide as many opportunities as possible. While basic training is important (skills training, on-the-job training), it is even more important that company leaders have access to leadership training.

The Walt Disney Company is very proud of Disney University (DU). It is not just a building...it also encompasses an overarching theme and belief system that employees and leaders are only as good as you allow them to be. The DU provides constant and on-going leadership development in areas such as management soft skills, organizational communication, strategic planning, and of course, Disney heritage and traditions.

Removing your employees from the operation to send them to training classes takes time. It takes creative scheduling. It takes flexibility. It takes teamwork for other areas to cover for you.

When I was a front desk manager at Port Orleans Resort-French Quarter, we would work closely with our peer group just down the Sassagoula River at Port Orleans Resort – Riverside. This allowed us to schedule leadership training with our front-line managers, while they sent some of their managers over to staff our shifts. We would always do the same for them. It's this type of partnership that allows everyone access to leadership development.

Disney believes that its high-performing leaders are going to want access to professional development. That could be instructor-led training, online learning, access to webinars, and professional conferences. Disney knows there is value in developing its leaders, and that is why it invests time, energy, and dollars into training its employees and leaders.

## Action Items

- Include leadership development dollars in your annual budget. If necessary, start with small dollar amounts.

- Work with your Human Resources teams to find ways to partner with other agencies to allow access to leadership development.

- Remember that a corporate university does not have to be a physical building – it can be a part of the culture.

# 2.

## Treat your Direct Reports as Valuable Assets

Managers and supervisors must spend time with their direct reports to encourage, inspire, and motivate. At Walt Disney World, this was one of my most important roles. With over 55,000 employees at the time, and hundreds of job opportunities for employees, it was important to discover the following about each of my direct reports:

- How can I help you excel in your current role?
- Where do you see yourself in the next two-three years?
- How can I help you get where you want to be?
- What do you need from me on a daily basis?

These questions were important to ask; the answers helped me map out a career growth strategy for each of my employees. Some wanted to move up in the resorts and become a general manager. Some wanted help moving over to the theme parks. Some were just at Disney for a couple of years for a line on their resume. Some knew they would be returning to a different state to live with members of their family. Some wanted to stay right where they were for the next 10 years.

All of those are valid goals...but I would not know about them if I did not ask.

We named my team of direct reports Pete's Pals. My co-managers also had fun names, like Fred's Friends and Darren's Dudes. We all created professional development binders with the names and information from the questions above for each of our 10-15 direct reports. We met with each of them formally for about one hour each quarter...more if they needed it.

Doing this lets the employees know that they were not just a number. They were not just a body that would be replaced when they leave. We wanted all our Cast Members to feel like they were part of a team with a leader who was looking out for their best interests.

Sometimes I had to share hard feedback. Sometimes I was privileged to be able to share the good news of a promotion or transfer opportunity. But my main goal, as a leader, was to take care of my employees so that they could focus on the most important part of their jobs...taking care of our guests.

### Action Items

- Create a schedule for meeting with your direct reports to talk about career growth.

- Talk with your fellow leaders about what they are doing with their teams, and emulate that when necessary.

- Be open and honest with your employees. Don't lead them down a path where there are no opportunities or where they will not be successful.

- Remember that it's OK if they leave. It's better to have employees leave if they don't want to be there.

# 3.
## Provide Regular One-on-One Meetings with your Direct Reports

So, what's the difference between scheduled one-on-one meetings and Pete's Pals meetings?

Simple.

Pete's Pals was specifically designed to discuss career growth. These were career development discussions so that I knew how to manage each person according to their short- and long-term career goals.

In addition (that's right...in addition) to these meetings, successful leaders also need to have regularly scheduled one-on-one meetings with their direct reports. My mentor at Disney drilled this into my head over and over. With so many Cast Members and a high amount of turnover, it was important to connect in a one-on-one fashion with each direct report.

**Topics in these meetings can include:**
- Current workload
- Asking for ideas on how to improve the area
- Constructive feedback on performance
- Positive feedback on performance
- Best practice sharing
- Asking about personal issues, such as family, kids, home life, etc.

Did that take a lot of time? Yes. But the payoff was immediate and immense. Each employee felt valued and knew that their supervisor/leader cared for them. They always went back to work in a better mood. They felt validated for what they felt and what they did.

Some managers at Disney relished in taking this extra step. While it was encouraged, it was not required. It was easy to tell the difference between employees that had these meetings and those that did not. Employees without leader feedback seemed a little more lost, forlorn, and unsettled. But those leaders that did have frequent one-on-one meetings saw a happier and more productive workforce.

## Action Items

- *Talk with each direct report and ask how often they would like to meet. Be reasonable and respectful of their needs.*

- *Have an agenda before each one-on-one so the conversation doesn't derail into a complaint session with no end in sight.*

- *Get buy-in from upper management. This type of leadership takes time, and they need to know how much time and effort you are putting into your employees.*

# 4.

# Harness the Power of Cross-Utilization

Cross-Utilization (Cross-U) is a staffing process that is designed to assist the Disney Parks during high volume days or weeks. Times such as Spring Break, July 4th week, and the week after Christmas were usually designated as times when the Cross-U program would go into effect.

The process is simple. All managers in non-parks and resorts roles were encouraged (read: required) to sign up for at least one Cross-U shift during these times. Those managers were usually in roles such as finance, HR, communications, administrative support, legal, risk management, marketing, public relations, and so on. There are two simple reasons for this program:

- Heavy crowds mean a higher need for Cast Members in custodial, queue management, guest services, food and beverage, and more. Having more employees working and visible during this time provides a better customer experience.
- Salaried Cast Members in backstage roles might lose focus of the main reason they work at Disney. Putting these employees back into a theme park role, even if only for half a workday, reminds them of the big picture and puts what they do into a clearer focus.

When I moved from Operations into Human Resources, I picked up many of these shifts over the course of my career. I held a wait time sign outside Space Mountain that read **Current Wait Time: 180 minutes** for four hours. I placed six pepperonis at a time on hundreds of individual-sized pizzas. I worked in Parade Audience Control (PAC) for multiple parades where one of my main responsibilities was telling our guests "I'm sorry, but this area is reserved for guests with disabilities."

The lessons I learned on these shifts stayed with me for my entire Disney career and beyond. It gave me credibility with other Cast Members. They appreciated seeing all the "suits" come out to the parks during these heavy times. But most of all, it kept me connected to what Walt Disney World was all about... creating an awesome guest experience.

### Action Items

- *Pick a time that you, as a leader, can take a front-line shift.*

- *Encourage other leaders who stay "backstage" to do the same. Pick up a phone shift in a call center, take a server shift in your restaurant, or greet customers at your entrance.*

- *Share your learnings and appreciation in a company newsletter or blog. Send thank-you notes or words of encouragement to those whose roles you experienced.*

# 5.

# Be Ready and Able to Jump in when needed

While Cross-U shifts were scheduled during heavy times, it was mostly designed for those managers/leaders that spent most of those days in their own offices or cubes. But what about the operational managers? What about those that are leading a team of people who are on the front-lines every day. What is the leader's role when the operation is busy?

There are two schools of thought to this.

Disney believes that leaders are leaders are leaders. Chances are fairly high that an operational manager (housekeeping, attractions, food and beverage, custodial, recreation, etc.) was promoted from within. They were most likely doing this work as a front-line employee before they were promoted.

I was working at Port Orleans Front Desk when I was promoted to a manager at Port Orleans Bell Services. I had no experience at all in bell services, but I learned it quickly. Many of my peers were promoted from a front desk role to management roles in Housekeeping or Food/Beverage. They, too, had NO experience in those areas, but Disney believed that a leader is a leader is a leader. If you were approachable, willing to learn, fair, company-focused, and motivating to others, then Disney can TEACH you the logistics of your new role (how to run a register, how to make a bed), so that you can jump in when needed to assist.

The other school of thought is that "you cannot lead me and manage me if you do not know exactly what I do and have done it yourself." I see this often in local government. There are managers who are great leaders, but they do not know all the technical ins and outs of their departments.

Therefore, they are not respected by their employees because they can't jump in and help when busy.

My personal opinion is that **they can**. The manager just needs to take a broader role when jumping in to assist. They can work the line, and ask who needs what. They can check paperwork. They can bring drinks and snacks to those waiting in line, and let the expert employees do what they do best.

In any event, you need to be ready as a leader to jump in and help when needed. It is the quickest way to gain the respect of your team. You don't have to know everything, and you **should** eventually learn everything when possible, but never stay back in your office when times get tight, lines get long, and bad things are happening. You need to jump right in.

## Action Items

- *Talk with your direct reports and find out how much they expect you to know about every role in the department and commit to learning as much as you can.*

- *Plan to jump in and help on those busy days to show your commitment to your employees.*

- *If you find yourself jumping in and helping more than you should be, it may be time to look at your processes, staffing, and strategic plan. Most leaders are paid to lead and manage, not to do the front-line work all the time. Have a plan in place to remedy this if necessary.*

# 6.

## Fix all Mistakes with a Guest-First Attitude

Problems come up at Disney all the time, just as they do in most organizations. Of all the companies I've worked for, I found that Disney wanted (encouraged) me to fix the problem with a guest-first attitude and not a me-first attitude. For example, when I checked a guest into a room that was not cleaned by the housekeeping staff, my goal was to get that guest moved into a clean room as soon as possible. Listed below are some steps and thoughts for this scenario based on both attitudes.

| Guest-First attitude | Me-First attitude |
| --- | --- |
| Apologize | Blame another department |
| Find a clean room right away | Find out why this happened – maybe the guest went to the wrong room. Grill the guest with questions. |
| Walk them to the room | Remind guest it was not your fault, but someone else's |
| Apologize again and offer service recovery as needed | Print them keys to a new room |
| Upon return to the front desk, research what happened and try to prevent in the future | Apologize |

Many of today's employees do not know how to solve problems. Using critical thinking skills to solve problems is an essential part of leadership.

Quick example. When my kids were growing up, I used to love watching them try to take something to the trash can in our kitchen. Especially when the trash can was full. They would take their paper plates or their napkins or a pizza to the trash can, open the lid to the trash can, look inside, see that it was too full, and then freeze. I would watch them stand there frozen like they had no idea what to do.

Most of the time their solution was to close the lid and place the garbage on top. I would comment from the kitchen that there had to be another solution. Then they would realize that they had to empty the garbage, put a new bag in, and take out the full bag. Problem solved. This is also a guest first attitude as it puts the needs of the next person who has garbage ahead of their own desire to just pile the garbage up on top and essentially pass the buck.

## Action Items

- *Ask others for help when you have a problem. Know that you don't know everything.*

- *Put your ego aside. A lot of people who choose not to solve problems or try to solve problems don't think that they can ask for help.*

- *Create a departmental culture where you fix the problem first, and examine the "why" behind the problem second.*

# 7.

# Learn and Live the Concept of Business Savvy

In the *Pirates of the Caribbean* movie franchise, Captain Jack Sparrow frequently uses the word "savvy" as a verb, meaning "understand?"

"Savvy" is also a noun, and it is an essential part of being a leader in the Disney organization. When used as a noun, it means shrewd and knowledgeable, and "the ability to make good judgments." That is a skill that Disney expects of all its leaders. There were seven core leadership competencies when I worked there, and one of them was to "demonstrate business savvy."

But what does that mean? What do you need to know to say you are business savvy?

- Do you know how to deal with the unwritten rules in your organization?
- Do you know how to play the office politics game?
- In a staff meeting, do you know when you can be more assertive versus when you can be silent?
- Do you know when you should ask questions?
- Do you know how to read a room?
- Do you know who the key players are?
- Do you understand the financial side of your operation?
- Do you know how to read a profit and loss statement or annual budget, no matter what your role?
- Do you read your annual report each year?
- Do you actively attempt to always learn more about the entire organization versus just living in your departmental bubble?

Being business savvy is more than just being the most technically competent person in your role. To maximize the value you can add in multiple areas, you have to care about the business as a whole and not just excel in your silo.

### Action Items

- *Are there any areas of your business where you could say "I have no idea what they do" or "I have no idea how they operate?" If so, schedule a 30-minute meeting, shadow, or overview of that department to learn more.*

- *Find a mentor in your organization who demonstrates business savvy. Watch how they act and behave in meetings and try to emulate those traits.*

- *Read your annual report every year, no matter how boring it may be.*

# 8.

# Act Like a Leader at all Times

My promotion to front desk manager at Disney's Port Orleans Resort meant that I was now leading others who were previously my peers. One night we thought that the front office manager had left for the day as it was about 7 o'clock PM. We started talking about belching. One of my employees said, "I'm the best belcher ever!" Because they were in a backstage area, they let out a tremendous belch.

Of course, I wanted to be one of the guys, so I released an even louder and bigger belch.

After the laughing subsided, people turned around to see the front office manager standing directly behind me. She pointed two fingers at me and said, "Pete, come to my office." The entire crowd let out a collective, "ooooooooooooh."

She spent 30 minutes talking with me about the importance of being a leader. She understood how I used to be a peer, and she understood my desire to still be connected to those people. But...she reminded me that as their leader, manager, and supervisor, I was now held to a higher standard.

I will never forget that talk, and I carried it over into my job in local government. I'll never forget being promoted after working side by side with a few of my trainers in Birmingham, Alabama. Within two months, one of the trainers came to me and said, "You've been acting a little differently and we want to make sure everything is OK."

That made me feel validated.

"I responded, "Yes, I am acting a little bit differently. I can't always make the same jokes and have the same camaraderie. We can still be friends and we can still work hard; we can still interact. But as a leader, there are certain things I have to do now." They appreciated that openness and honesty.

This holds true for you as well. Never forget that as a leader you are held to a higher standard, and your behavior and actions must always accompany that. Failure to do so will result in the loss of respect and integrity from your direct reports.

## Action Items

- *Are there any negative traits or behaviors that you have as a supervisor that you should change?*

- *Talk with your employees and let them know what your role is as a leader.*

- *Check with your fellow supervisors and ask them if you have any behaviors that seem too inappropriate or too chummy. Ask them how you can better model leadership behaviors to help your department and your career as part of your personal and your professional development.*

# 9.

# Share your Expectations with your Direct Reports within their First Week

The Walt Disney Company does a great job communicating expectations with its employees on Day One. Disney has a "Traditions" orientation class where all new Cast Members spend a day and a half at the Disney University learning about the history, heritage, and expectations of the company. Later that week, the new hires are taken to their local areas where they first meet with their direct supervisor. It is at this time that the supervisor sits down with the employees and shares their expectations as their leader.

Every supervisor is different. Every manager has different expectations. It is imperative that you, as a supervisor and leader, share those expectations with your employees on the first day that you meet with them. I try to do this with all of my new employees at least within their first week. This includes all the standard rules, regulations, policies, and procedures. But then I share my own personal expectations.

These may go above and beyond what the company expects. These may be my own personal expectations that help my employees understand who I am as a leader, where my values are, and what I expect. Here are some examples.

- I tell my employees that I expect them to work hard and not be clock watchers.
- I don't expect them to tell me when they work 10 minutes late or leave 10 minutes early, but I do expect them to work hard at all times and be available.

- I expect my employees to ask everybody if they want something for lunch when they leave for lunch. That way when they come back with a bag of food, the other employees don't look at them and say, "Oh, I wish you would have asked me."
- I expect them to be transparent and work as a team.
- I expect them to share everything that they want me to know and I'll share everything with them that I want them to know.
- I expect them to always act and behave according to our values.

Never let your employees say "I didn't know what to expect from you" or "I don't know what's expected of me in this job." While you should always share the technical expectations that you have of them, it's just as important for you to share the leadership expectations as well.

## Action Items

- *Set aside one hour to share your expectations with your employees and hear what their expectations are of you during their first week of training.*

- *Have a list of your expectations ready to go.*

- *Check with other department managers who are your peers and find out if they do the same thing. You want to make sure that your departmental expectations align for all employees while keeping in mind that each supervisor may have different individual expectations of their direct reports. You don't want to cause any inconsistency in your department.*

# 10.

# Have Awareness beyond your own Department

This one is so important that former Executive Vice-President Lee Cockerell listed this as one of his great leader strategies: "Know what is going on in your organization." One of my many roles at Disney was that of a front desk manager. That meant that I needed to know everything about check in's, check-outs, arrival times, budgets, scheduling, and everything else that had to do with a front desk environment in a resort hotel.

But the learning did not stop there. Disney also expected me to know as much as I could about the recreation department, the custodial department, the housekeeping department, the food and beverage department, and so on. They also expected me to know what was happening at Epcot, the Magic Kingdom, Disney-MGM Studios and Disney's Animal Kingdom. I did not work at any of those locations, but the expectation for me, as a leader, was that I did not work in a silo, and so I tried to learn a little about every location and role.

How does this apply to you in your organization? Great leaders need to know what's going on in the entire organization...not only what's happening in their department.

- Do you know what's happening in other areas of your company?
- Do you know the opening and closing times of different departments?
- Do you have contacts you can call to get that information?

Lots of times, I was asked questions and my answer could be "I don't know - that's not my department." But I pride myself and my team on saying "This is the information we have," and then sharing it with them because we've done the research. Also, if we don't know, we'll use the common Disney phrase, "I don't know, but let me find out for you." (or "let's find out together.")

The sign of a great leader, as I learned at Disney, is to always know what's going on in your organization. Great leaders never stand back and say "I didn't see that coming, "I didn't know that was going to happen," or "That's a whole different department from me. How should I know?"

Great leaders know.

## Action Items

- Make a list of all the departments where you need to learn more.

- Set up one-on-ones with the managers of those departments to have 15 to 30-minute overviews to understand their business, learn what they do, and ask how your department can help their department.

- Never say "I don't know" or "That's not my job." Pride yourself and pride your entire team on having as much information as you can about every area of your organization.

# 11.

## Be a Leadership R.O.L.E. Model

The leadership team at Disney always preached the difference between your purpose and your role. All Cast Members had the same purpose (create happiness by providing the finest in entertainment for people of all ages), but their roles were all different. The goal of leadership was to make sure each employee knew how their role (job) fit into the overall purpose of Disney.

While Disney believes that everyone can be a leader, there are certain obligations and behavioral patterns that really strong leaders exhibit. Working at Disney led me to create what I call the Leadership R.O.L.E. Model. To me, employees were always looking for role models to assist with their personal and professional success. After years of on-the-job research at Disney and in government, I believe that high-performing leaders should exhibit the following traits and behaviors:

### (R)elationships

It may not be what you know or who you know, in the end, it's all about who knows you! Great leaders establish great relationships with individuals, other departments, and other people outside of work.

### (O)versight

The outdated concept of oversight is **big brother is watching** and **micromanagement**. My definition of oversight is **watchful care**. Great leaders have watchful care over both their physical property and their employees.

### (L)everage

Leverage is the ability to influence people, events, and decisions. Great leaders leverage their position, their personality, and their partnerships to make positive changes at work.

### (E)volvement

Great leaders never stop learning. The day you decide you know everything should be the day that you retire.

### Action Items

- *Build (R)elationships by volunteering for projects at work that no one else wants.*

- *Build (O)versight by showing you care about your people, property, and processes.*

- *Build (L)everage by offering help to others before asking for it yourself.*

- *Build (E)volvement by setting professional development goals each year.*

# 12.

# Make Employee Recognition a Top Priority

I learned so much about recognition from working at Walt Disney World. This organization taught me that recognizing your employees for good work will pay incredible dividends. On the other hand, constantly criticizing your employees can cost your organization money, customers, and brand image. Yes, you have to coach, develop, and give constructive feedback. Yes, leaders have to have one-on-ones to develop their employees. But we spend so much time trying to find the bad and what people are doing wrong and how to correct their mistakes, that we forget to thank them and recognize them for the hard work they do each and every day.

As a leader at Disney, I was handed an orange box called the Disney recognition toolkit. In it were books on how to recognize employees, a calendar for every day to remind you how to recognize your employees, helpful hints on how to recognize your employees, best practices from other departments on how to recognize your employees, and so on.

In contrast, when I arrived at my role in local government, there was very little structure around recognition. Everybody worked off the assumption that people were getting paid and that's recognition enough. There was a pervasive thought that employees do not need to be thanked for doing their job. It is true that some employees do not need or want to be thanked for going above and beyond. They just work hard and go above and beyond because that is who they are. But those employees in today's environment are few and far between. Every employee needs to be told "good job!", recognized with a gift card, mentioned on the bulletin board to showcase their good work, or spoken about positively in a team meeting.

Make sure that you are actively recognizing your employees so they can add value to your customers' experience with your organization.

### Action Items

- *Put a structure in place for your department or organization around the how, when, and why of recognition.*

- *Always encourage immediate, off-the-cuff recognition above and beyond your formalized recognition structure.*

- *Talk with your employees and find out how each one of them likes to be recognized, and then personalize it for each of them. Remember, some employees would be uncomfortable if you recognized them in a public forum.*

# 13.

# Place the Right Employees into the Right Jobs for the Right Reasons

When I worked at Walt Disney World, I was invited to take part in a management development program titled the Disney Leadership Development Program (DLDP). It was created to look at high performers and their skill sets and place them in a management intern role.

Some of us were placed in housekeeping. Some of us were placed in food and beverage. Some of us were placed in attractions or custodial.

The DLDP selection committee attempted to put us in what they thought were the best-fit roles for us. The same principle applies to you as a leader. You need to look at your individual team members and decide if they are in the right fit role.

- If you have somebody working at the front counter, do they have extraversion skills?
- If you had someone working in finance or accounting, are they OK working with numbers all day?
- If you have someone who likes working with people, do you have them in a cube all by themselves or do they have team interaction?

Disney is big on putting you in a right-fit role. For example, I moved from a Magic Kingdom Parking Host to an Attractions Host to a Front Desk Host to Bell Services Manager to a Traditions Facilitator to a Performance Consultant to a Segment Learning Manager. There were certain parts of each role that were right-fit for me, and there were other parts that I had to learn. My final role at Disney as a Segment Learning Manager was truly a right-fit role.

This concept of right-fit is a little bit different in government. There, when you put somebody into a certain role, it's hard to move them out due to certain rules, regulations, and policies. But if you have the capability to keep a high performer who may be in a wrong-fit role, see if you can move them around your organization instead of terminating them. Is there a better fit for them in a different department? Is there a right-fit role for them somewhere else in your organization? See if you can keep them and put them somewhere else so they can continue to add value.

### Action Items

- *Look at all of your direct reports and decide if they are in a right-fit role.*

- *If they are, have a conversation with them to validate that they are engaged in their jobs.*

- *If they are not in a right-fit role, look around your organization to find roles that might be better suited for them, and see if you can move them to somewhere else.*

# 14.

## Communicate the Overall Purpose of every Role

When I worked at Disney's Port Orleans Resort, I had a resident manager by the name of Vince. It was the first time I had ever heard the following phrase:

*"The main thing is keeping the main thing the main thing."*

Everyone who worked with Vince knew what he meant. He was telling us that no matter what our "job" was, we should never forget our purpose, as that is the main thing. It was to make sure that every guest had the most fantastic vacation of their lives. It did not matter if you were in housekeeping, recreation, front desk, food and beverage, or management. We all knew that each of our roles contributed to the purpose of the organization.

In fact, during Disney Traditions (which is the first-day orientation program for all new Cast Members), everyone is told of the overall purpose of Walt Disney World:

*"We create happiness by providing the finest in family entertainment for people of all ages, everywhere."*

Do your employees know what the "main thing" is in your organization? All employees have daily tasks that they have to accomplish, and all of them have checklists and things to do. But at the end of the day, can all of your employees safely say that they are speaking from the same playbook?

It does not matter what industry you're in. You need to make sure that every single employee knows that the **overall purpose** of their role is more important than the **daily tasks** of their role.

## Action Items

- *Do you have an overarching purpose statement that you can share with all of your employees?*

- *Make sure that your overall purpose is shared in your orientation class on day one to every single new employee.*

- *Make sure that employees know the difference between the purpose statement and their regular tasks. Remind them that their tasks are important, but their purpose keeps the company in business, provides lifelong customers, and allows them to provide unparalleled service.*

# 15.

# Hire for Attitude and Train for Skill

The Walt Disney World Resort has a beautiful themed building called the Casting Center. Future Cast Members will enter the doors and head through the small rotunda filled with statues of famous Disney characters, just before they slowly make their way up a gently sloping ramp to the top floor, where they are greeted by a friendly Cast Member who will assist them on their career journey.

Let me share with you what does NOT happen.

Potential Cast Member: *"Hi. My name is Pete, and I am an expert in selling popcorn. I have worked in multiple theme parks and amusement parks popping, buttering, and serving popcorn. I have sold thousands of boxes of popcorn, and I want to be a part of the popcorn community here at Disney."*

Disney: *"Fantastic. You are just what we are looking for! You are hired."*

Disney strives to hire people who are nice, friendly, and outgoing. They want Cast Members who love the company, are self-starters, and are good team players. If you happen to be good at popcorn, that is a bonus.

Disney can train you how to sell popcorn. They can't train you to have a better attitude.

The same holds true in your organization. Yes, there are certain jobs that require a certain skill set, like an airline pilot, accountant, and chief engineer. You can't hire those folks on their positive attitude alone. But for those customer-facing roles such as baggage handler, accounting assistant, and engineering support, you might do well to hire those who have great attitudes. Then if you need to, you can spend a few dollars to train them.

Hire for attitude and train for skill when you can. It will save you a lot of headaches down the road.

### Action Items

- *Does your interview process take attitude into account? Work with your HR department to include non-discriminatory questions that try to measure attitude.*

- *Are there employees in your department that have the technical skills, but have bad attitudes? See if you can pinpoint why, and do what you can to allow them to adapt before you have to help them move on to greener pastures.*

- *Reward those employees who always display a positive attitude. A simple "Thank you for always being positive" can go a long way.*

# 16.

## Promote from within whenever possible

Whenever possible, Walt Disney World Resort tried to promote approximately 80 percent of our managers from the front-line Cast. Promoting from within leads to higher morale. The higher your employee's morale, the better the engagement and the better succession plan you have.

There is real power in a culture that encourages internal promotions. It creates better camaraderie and better teamwork. Employees know that managers have walked in their shoes. They respect that manager. A manager that comes in from the outside doesn't understand "how we do things around here," and they may have a hard time acclimating into the culture.

When you work at Walt Disney World as a front-line Cast Member, you may have...

- cleaned bathrooms over and over again.
- talked to angry guests over and over.
- given the same safety spiel over 100 times a day, every day.

Managers who have been promoted from the front-lines tend to understand what the front-line Cast is going through.

Now, this may not work in every organization. There are some organizations where skilled crafts and trades are needed in order to work in a leadership or management position. But my history and my experience tell me that if you create a culture that encourages internal promotions, those employees that want to move up in the organization see a culture where that happens. Then work even harder to achieve their goals.

Bonus: Having employees in leadership roles that also have experienced the front line will benefit both the employee and the organization.

## Action Items

- *What percentage of your employees who are in management are promoted from within? Capture that data and share it as a recruiting tool.*

- *Let your employees know what succession planning looks like in your organization. Make them aware of the classes they need, the people with which they need to network, and the skills they need in order to get promoted.*

- *Share success stories of employees who have been promoted throughout your organization. Showcase them in newsletters or in recruiting guides so that others know that you are a company that values internal promotions.*

# Section Two

## The Magic of the
# Employees

*Do you want to be the best employee you can be?
Whether you are a manager, supervisor,
or individual contributor, these chapters
will help you add magic to your everyday work.*

# 17.

# Learn to "Love your Job"

I created the JOBS Model of Employee Engagement after I realized there were four main factors that lead to employee engagement. An employee could love their job, love their organization, love their boss (manager or supervisor), or love their squad (their teammates).

The Disney Company wants all of its employees to love their job. The term "job" could have different meanings. It could be your position, your title, or your role. But at the end of the day, Disney encourages all of its employees to love the **daily tasks** that are associated with their current roles.

For example, have you ever heard statements like this?

- **Nursing** – "This job would be great if it wasn't for all the patients."
- **Finance** – "This job would be perfect if I didn't have to sit in a cube all day."
- **Public Safety** – "This would be the most awesome job if it wasn't for all the calls we get."

Those are part of the **everyday tasks** for those jobs. "Love your Job" is all about the employee coming to terms with the daily tasks of their role and learning to love and appreciate those daily tasks.

Walt Disney World is no different from those jobs listed above. A merchandise host or hostess has to stock shelves and process sales at the register. An attractions host has to load attractions, say "watch your step" thousands of times a day, and share safety spiels. A custodial host must clean bathrooms, sweep trash, and clean up "protein spills" throughout the parks on a daily basis.

There are some fun tasks that come with these roles: for example, having guest interactions that place smiles on guests faces is fun. Having very little micromanagement and being able to be creative in the guest service roles are fun. BUT...employees that love their job (including those daily, repetitive tasks) will find themselves happier and more fulfilled than those who resent the day-to-day tasks that come with every job in every company.

## Action Items

- *Find a way to put some fun in the daily, monotonous tasks. Can you turn those tasks into a daily competition with others? Can you find a way to perform them that is different from others (e.g., how Southwest Airlines delivers their safety spiels?)*

- *Decide if you are in a right-fit role. Perhaps the daily tasks demotivate you because you are not in a role that maximizes the use of all your talents. Set up a one-on-one with your supervisor to find out if there are other roles/jobs where you can transfer or promote into which would be a better fit.*

- *Remind yourself that the grass is not always greener. Every job and every role have daily tasks that must be completed. Positive self-talk may help you love the daily tasks with your job.*

# 18.

# Learn to "Love your Organization"

The Disney organization has a history and tradition that allows employees to fall in love with it. Learning to love your organization is all about discovering what you love most about your company. Examples may include pay, work-life balance, insurance and benefits, recognition programs, retirement options, casual dress, employee perks, vacation and sick leave, an employee-first culture, free parking, and so on. Disney constantly reminds its employees about all the good things that come with working for Disney.

When I first started at Disney, the free admission to the parks was a huge benefit for me and my family, and it solidified my appreciation for the company. I also loved the fact that my sole purpose every day was to be part of a company that wanted to "create happiness by providing the finest in family entertainment for people of all ages everywhere." With an overarching goal like that, it's easy to love your organization.

I understand that not everyone works for a company like Disney...but that doesn't mean that employees don't want to be a part of something bigger. I knew many employees who did not like the job they were doing, or maybe had a bad supervisor, but...they loved the Disney Company and all it had to offer...and that was good enough for them.

Employees who love their organizations become brand ambassadors for the company. They don't like it where there is bad press, and they take it personally when there are negative reviews on Yelp or TripAdvisor about their company. "Love your Organization" is about appreciating everything your company is doing for you, telling others all about it, and navigating the ups and downs of business knowing that you are proud of where you work.

## Action Items

- Take a moment and make a list of all the things you love about your organization, and include tangible and intangible benefits. Let your supervisor or CEO know how much you appreciate all the good things that your company offers its employees.

- Ask others in your community what they think of when they hear your company name? Do their answers validate how you feel, or is the public perception of the company different from how you feel and what you believe? If it is different, what can you do to improve it?

- Remember that no organization is perfect, and there is no utopian company that offers a perfect workplace.

# 19.

# Learn to "Love your Boss"

Many employees at Disney love their job, and many more love their organization. It is also true that a great many of these employees also love their boss.

This is something in which Disney takes great pride. When I worked at Disney University, my role was Segment Learning and Development Manager. Our team was tasked with providing professional and career development training for the Cast Members at Walt Disney World, Disneyland, and Disney Cruise Line. An essential part of our training and development opportunities centered on leadership development.

This is a no-brainer. If you do not develop your front-line managers, your employee morale is destined to drop. If you do not train your front-line leaders, your employee base will revolt against those bad leaders. Front-line leadership development was understood to be just as valuable as customer service training, safety training, and every other type of training.

Thus, Disney has many employees who have great relationships with their direct supervisor. There may be Cast Members who are not big fans of the company, and may not be in love with their day-to-day role, but they love their boss. They would follow them anywhere. In fact, high-performing front-line leaders are often transferred to different disciplines (attractions to custodial, food and beverage to operations, merchandise to recreation) to allow them to learn a new line of business, grow in the company, and set themselves up for future success.

When these transfers happen, it is not uncommon for their direct reports to plead, "Take me with you!" Some employees would rather transfer to a less appealing job in order to stay with a leader who motivates and inspires them.

Organizations that focus on leadership development and make it a priority will, in turn, see employees who love working there based on the great relationships they make with their supervisor. That, in turn, means many more employees who will love their boss.

## Action Items

- *Grade your current relationship with your supervisor using the scale A-F. If you have an A, let your current leader know how much you appreciate them. If you have a B-F, set up a time to have a vulnerable, transparent conversation with your supervisor to share your feelings. Don't tell them what they need to do for you...instead, ask them what you can do to help improve the relationship. Take the first step.*

- *Find out what leadership development programs exist or are offered by your company. Enroll in any training classes or sessions that are available, even if you think you don't need them. The day you stop learning at your company should be retirement day.*

- *If you currently "love your boss," use him or her as a role model for when you take on a management or leadership role. Emulate your boss to enhance your future success.*

# 20.

# Learn to "Love your Squad"

Do you love the current team to which you are assigned? To many employees, this may be the one item that is keeping them engaged at work. Perhaps you don't love your job, your organization, or your boss... but the people you work with every day make you laugh, make you smile, and make you want to come to work every day.

That is what "Love your Squad" is all about.

The Gallup Organization has been using its Q12 employee engagement survey for years, and one of the 12 rating statements is, "I have a best friend at work." Their research shows that folks who have friends at work usually have higher engagement scores.

Keep in mind that this engagement concept may not be for everyone. Some employees have no desire to have close friends at work. They want to come to work, do their job well, and then go home. They have other outlets for friends/relationships, such as professional organizations, church, or even their neighborhoods. But for others, this is a huge part of their work. Many employees understand that they spend more time at work than they do at home, and therefore having friends at work is a key driver for them.

Disney understands that. They do not try to squash relationships. In fact, making friends at work is encouraged. They know that when employees form teams, they will most likely cover for each other, support each other, and add value for the guests. This is so much better than teams that backstab each other, gossip about each other, and injure each other as they try to climb the corporate ladder.

Whether it is team building events or allowing employees to go on break at the same time so they can talk, Disney understands that if Cast Members love their squad, the results to the bottom line are bound to be positive.

### Action Items

- *How important is it for you to have friends at work? If you are not getting the peer relationships you desire, talk with your supervisor about your needs and how they can assist.*

- *If your leader does not create team-friendly events, take matters into your own hands. What can you do to create some fun, no-cost events at work (chili cookoff in the Fall, Summer hot dog party, lunch walk to a local museum, etc.)?*

- *Be aware of those who do not need to love their squad. Don't make others feel like outcasts just because they have outside friends. Always include everyone and let them decide if and how they want to participate.*

# 21.
# Utilize Intrinsic Motivation over Insurmountable Money

Cast Members working the front-line roles at Disney Theme Parks and Resorts are not going to get rich. In fact, many Cast Members may have second jobs in order to make ends meet. This is not a discussion starter to talk about the pros and cons of CEOs as millionaires, income redistribution, or $15 minimum wages. The point is simple. You will never make what you think you are worth.

- If you make $15/hour, you think you should be making $20/hour.
- If you make $50,000/year, you think you should be making $60,000/year.
- If you make $1.5 million/year, you think you are worth $2.0 million/year.

This is because someone else is always making more than you, and you think you work harder in your position than they do.

Disney knows this, understands this, and realizes they may not be able to win employee loyalty on salary alone. Part of the job of the human resource department (HR) is to share the total benefits package with employees, and let them see when you add up salary, insurance, benefits, park admission, discounted lunches, free parking, and so on, and so on, you are making more than just your hourly wage.

While this will satisfy some employees, most Disney Cast Members have learned the value of intrinsic motivation. Most people who work at Disney will not list "money" as one of the reasons they work there. In fact, many long-time Disney Cast Members have stayed despite the fact that they could make more money in a different company.

But there is something magical about working for Disney. It is almost like a calling. For some, it is no different from those who are called to ministry, social work, health care, and public safety. Many in those fields do not make a lot of money, yet they stay and do great work. The power of self-motivation is too great to ever leave.

Successful companies will make sure that their employees know that money should not be a key driver of happiness. Being paid a legitimate wage is important...but it cannot be the only driver of employee engagement.

## Action Items

- Ask yourself if you would leave your current company if a competitor offered you 5% more? 10% more? What if it came with more money, but longer work hours?

- Do you feel connected to the mission/vision/values of your company? If not, why not? If yes, why does that make you stay?

- Ask employees with the longest seniority why they stayed? Perhaps create a video blog showcasing your high performing, longtime employees sharing how it is "not all about the money." Use this video as a retention strategy to keep those who may be looking around for reasons to leave.

## 22.

# Create a Successful Recognition Program

It is important for any organization to take a long, hard look at their recognition programs. The Disney organization has a very strong and very powerful recognition program. If you want to inspire your employees, it is very important to have a great recognition program.

To begin, there needs to be a peer-to-peer recognition program. Disney had what was called the "Guest Service Fanatic" (GSF) card in which employees could recognize each other. It was nothing more than an index-sided card that was available to all Cast Members. When a Cast Member saw someone at work go above and beyond, they would recognize them with this card. Cast Members would even carry these cards when they went to the theme parks as guests. These cards would be forwarded to management so that those employees would be recognized, and it would be documented in their personnel file. Prizes were also awarded at staff meetings to encourage employees to recognize each other!

This is a great way for peer-to-peer recognition. There is always a fear that employees will take advantage of this and unethically reward each other, but if you make sure that what they write down is detailed and has all the correct information, then it can be very successful. No one is going to write down "Pete smiled at someone today" and give them a GSF card.

People are going to use it correctly because sometimes managers are too busy to notice the little things.

The second thing you have to do is create a formalized recognition program. At Disney, it is part of the Disney Difference. This can be managers receiving recognition toolboxes when they're promoted into management to know exactly how to recognize employees. This can be pins and plaques that are assigned and presented every year. This can be annual celebrations where you take your high performing employees out to meals.

The more it's formalized, and the more employees know about it, the more they want to work hard to achieve certain goals. With the advent of technology, a lot of this can be done electronically. Always look for ways to creatively recognize your employees.

## Action Items

- Take a good, hard look at your recognition programs, both in your organization and in your department. Do you know what is available to recognize people?

- Let your employees know all the details surrounding your formal and informal recognition programs.

- Dismiss the fact that you may be old school and believe that "a hard day's work for a hard day's pay" is all people need. In this day and age, it's important to know that people want more than just a thank you. In the war for talent, it's important that your organization has a recognition program in place to keep your high performers from leaving.

# 23.

## Look for a Right-Fit Role

There is nothing more magical to an employee than being placed in a right-fit role. A right-fit role does not mean that you meet the minimum qualifications. It does not mean that you have all the technical skills. A right-fit role means you look at the entirety of the person, the entirety of the role, and the entirety of the department, and then try and create what's called a right-fit.

For example, at Disney, we have employees who are both introverts and extroverts. A right-fit role for an extrovert means you try to place them in a role where they can get their energy from other people; this can be fellow Cast member or guests. Similarly, while many introverts can succeed in guest-facing roles, it is important for leadership to make sure they will be more productive there versus in a low guest-demand area.

Other things to consider when trying to place people in right-fit roles include personality, skill sets, talents, hobbies and more. It may involve looking at their family structure, their work-life balance, where they are in life, what they're trying to accomplish, who they might be working with as part of a departmental culture. This takes a lot of work between human resources, recruiting, and the individual leader.

There are many employees at Disney who started their careers in wrong-fit roles. They did the job to the best of their ability and waited, networked, talked to people, and worked with their leader until they could find a right-fit role for them. Sometimes we look at an employee who may not be performing and we decide it's time for them to move on. Rather than try and move them out of the organization, Disney teaches us all to try and find a right-fit role for each employee. Now, this may be more difficult in government or small organizations, but the concept remains the same. Employees working in right-fit roles show higher retention, have higher engagement levels, and add more value to your bottom line.

## Action Items

- *What are the parameters around a right-fit role in your mind? Have you ever thought of this concept? Brainstorm what right-fit skills are needed for your department.*

- *Which of your employees would you consider to be in a wrong-fit role? Are you in a wrong-fit role right now? What can you do to have a conversation to move beyond it and into a different role?*

- *Does your organization have existing rules, regulations, or policies that prevent employees from transferring or moving into right-fit roles? What can you do to improve that process?*

# 24.

# Take advantage of Professional Development Opportunities

When I was at Disney, the opportunities for professional learning and development were plentiful. Through the magic of Disney University, there were always training classes on professional development, leadership development, computer skills, and Disney history. In addition to that, small conferences were always available. Disney University created a multiday event called the Disney Leadership Conference, which was an onsite event for managers and leaders in the Disney organization. This allowed us to bring many speakers and internal subject matter experts into one location. This event was held at Disney's Contemporary Resort and allowed the employees to cover for each other while different employees attended the conference on different days.

Here's the key.

If you are a leader or manager in your organization, you need to make sure that you provide professional development opportunities for your employees. There needs to be some money put into the budget for this. There needs to be low-cost, no-cost opportunities for people to get better at a skill, at a trade, or at a leadership competency level.

If you are an employee and your organization offers professional development, you **must** take advantage of it. You must communicate with your leader how valuable you believe it to be. Believe it or not, there are some organizations that offer professional development and training, yet many employees choose not to take advantage of it. Upper management may see that no one takes an interest, and they take those dollars and allocate them for other areas. This defeats the entire purpose of professional development.

It can also affect the morale and engagement of those employees who do desire this type of learning and aren't able to get it.

Make sure that you **provide** professional development opportunities and **attend** those that are available for you.

## Action Items

- Make a comprehensive list of everything you want to learn to get better in your job.

- Talk with your leader about professional development opportunities. There are always low-cost or no-cost opportunities such as Fred Pryor Seminars or National Training Seminars. If you have a corporate university, take advantage of all their offerings.

- If you are a manager or CEO, make sure that professional development and continual training are a part of your overall culture. Include it in your budget each year to show employees how much you value them.

# 25.

# Allow Creativity and Innovation to Flourish

Walt Disney World once had a innovation-capturing concept called "I Have an Idea." The process was simple: Mini-mailboxes were placed throughout the property, and any Cast Member who had an idea on how to make the company, the organization, or their department better could fill out a card and drop it into those boxes. Those ideas that were used and implemented would be recognized by leadership and given a small prize such as a $25-dollar gift card.

Of course, Disney soon realized they were in the intellectual property business, and they had to stop this process after employees started putting in ideas for roller coasters, themed restaurants and things like that. But the point remains valid…

Do your employees have an opportunity to share their ideas with your organization?

Creativity and innovation are what make organizations successful. These allow employees to think beyond just their daily tasks and to add value to organizations with their creativity. Let your employees know as soon as they start working with you that their creative juices are not limited to their own department. If they have an idea that they think will help the overall organization, invite them to share it with their supervisor or manager so that they can become a part of the creative culture.

## Action Items

- *Let employees be creative and innovative on a regular basis. Share with them the expectations of how to share their creative ideas.*

- *Read Daniel Pink's book called Drive and learn about the concept of autonomy. People love to be creative in the ways that they do their work, and they love to be autonomous.*

- *When applicable, provide some type of recognition when creative and innovative solutions are implemented, especially those that save your company money.*

## 26.

# Showcase your Employee Success Stories

The Walt Disney Company loves to share stories of their employees doing great work, and you can model this strategy as well. This is a great way for you and your organization to improve employee morale and provide incredible internal customer service.

One way Disney did it was called "My Disney Career." This concept included a full day expo, a web application that shared information about employees, newsletter and newspaper articles about employees, and more. The expo consisted of a full day led by employees who had been promoted in their current role. Those employees would host an expo booth at a centralized location where other employees who wanted to transfer into other locations could go and talk with them. This allowed employees to hear directly from front-line employees what it's like to work in attractions, food and beverage, or custodial. They could talk about how they moved up through the organization. They could talk about all the good things you can do with the company.

In addition, employee success stories can be shared, recognizing those employees who volunteer in the community, win awards, graduate from college, or more. Employees love to see other employees doing good work, and they love to recognize and respect each other. If you truly want to motivate and inspire your employees, make sure that you showcase the great things your employees are doing. Use social media channels, newsletters, or perhaps an all-day expo.

## Action Items

- *Find out if a communication plan exists based on the successes of your employees.*

- *Create a committee to collect examples of employee successes, or create an online portal where employees can self-nominate themselves or others who they know are doing great things.*

- *Share these great stories about your company with outside organizations, newsletters, newspapers, social media, and the like. This will help build your organization's brand and make your employees proud to work for you.*

# 27.

........................

# Create a Fun Work Environment

Make work fun. There...I said it. This is going to rub some people the wrong way, but it is vital to the success of your organization.

Work has to be fun.

These days, the war for talent is unending and will continue to cause organizations to fight for the best people. Social media has allowed for immediate communication about the good and bad of your company. New benefits and work situations, such as flextime, are able to be shared immediately, becoming ammunition in the talent war. Therefore, it is imperative that you create a fun workplace to use as a differentiator in recruiting and retention.

Disney, by nature of its offerings, was always a fun place to work. You can do it too. Here are just a few examples of things you can do to create a fun workplace:

- Institute first-Friday breakfasts.
- Create chili cookoff events.
- Implement a fun monthly competition based on sales, outputs, etc.
- Allow employees to decorate their desks for the holidays.
- Create some type of costume contest when applicable (and follow all HR laws).
- Present fun skits to explain new policies.
- Have the CEO start every board meeting with a joke of the day.
- Take your team on field trips to local organizations.
- Play games during lunch.
- Have a college football kickoff event.

- Have a 4th of July event or any other holiday celebrations.
- Have people cook hot dogs one day for lunch.

All of these ideas are simple, low cost, or no-cost ways to make the workplace more fun.

**Action Items**
- *Don't look here for them. They are all listed above!*

## 28.

# Choose to be Engaged instead of Disengaged

For many years, the Gallup Organization has been measuring employee engagement levels and their impact on organizations. I love their research due to the simplicity of it. They categorize employees into three different levels: Engaged, Not Engaged (formerly known as Disengaged) and Actively Disengaged.

2019 saw the highest percentage of "engaged" workers (35%) in the U.S. since Gallup began tracking this metric in 2000. The 2019 numbers were as follows:

- Engaged             35%
- Not Engaged         52%
- Actively Disengaged 13%

I've been using these Gallup engagement statistics in my training sessions for years, and these percentages have been fairly consistent, give or take a few percentage points here and there.

Team members with higher levels of engagement are known to produce better outcomes, treat customers better and attract new ones, and are more likely to remain with their organizations than those who are less engaged. (Source:http://www.gallup.com/workplace/284180/factors-driving-record-high-employee-engagement.aspx)

Disney knows this. This is why they do everything they can to try and keep their employees engaged. But the company (and ANY company) can only do so much. In my opinion, it will always fall onto the employee to decide if they want to be engaged at work.

As an employee, it is up to you. It will always be up to you.

Make sure that you choose a job/career/company that excites you, motivates you, aligns with your personal values, and allows to you add value every single day.

It's not up to the organization.

It's up to you.

## Action Items

- *Learn more about the Gallup Organization and review their research on the concept of employee engagement.*

- *Get to know those employees in your workplace who you know have high levels of engagement. Take time to talk to them and ask them what drives them every day.*

- *Keep your personal engagement levels high regardless of any external circumstances. Good things come to those who are engaged at work no matter the economic climate.*

# Section Three

## The Magic of the
# Customer Experience

*Do you want your customer service to be amazing?
Do you have a passion for creating a customer
service experience as magical as Disney?*

**Then this is the section for you!**

## 29.

# Make Eye Contact with your Guests

It's a very simple concept that's trained and taught to all Disney Cast Members.

Make eye contact with each and every guest.

It helps to build a bond, or even build a relationship with a guest. It's the start of building a level of trust with them. Disney teaches that every interaction could be a potential future customer. At Disney, every employee is "onstage" when there are guests present.

In your organization, this could also include when you are off the clock. Do your employees wear logo shirts? Do they stop at the grocery store on the way home? If so, they are still "onstage." They could be coming in contact with a current or future customer. That is why the power of eye contact is so important.

Today's customer seems to always be looking down (at their phone) versus looking straight ahead, and that is why making eye contact and smiling when possible is so important. Smiles are becoming a lost art. That person may not know who you are, but they will know that the person in the "insert business here" logo shirt looked at them and smiled.

Making eye contact not easy. It seems uncomfortable. That is why Disney puts such a high priority on it. It's almost becoming an organizational differentiator to make eye contact with people. If you want to increase your customer service scores, gain more business, and stand out from your competition, you will want to make this a non-negotiable trait for all your employees. If Disney thinks it's good enough to take care of their guests by making eye contact and smiling, then it must be a good idea.

Who knows? It might even create an environment where employees start making eye contact and smiling at each other. Wouldn't that be great?

### Action Items

- *Do some internet research on the power of smiling and eye contact and share that knowledge in a team meeting.*

- *Include "make eye contact" or "provide smiles at all times" as part of your non-negotiable customer service standards.*

- *Include a short training message or video on this from the CEO.*

# 30.

# Provide a Welcoming Greeting

Disney trains its employees to greet and welcome each and every guest. You don't assume the Cast Member behind you is going to do it, and you don't assume that the Cast Member in front of you is going to do it. If you see a guest coming toward you, you use phrases such as "welcome," "hello," "good morning," "good afternoon," or "nice to see you!" Anything...as long as it is a greeting.

When I worked at Disney's Port Orleans Resort– French Quarter, I spent many shifts standing outside the main lobby under the Porte Cochere talking with guests. Those that drove up in their car who were arriving to check-in were easy to greet. These guests were easy to talk with and welcome. Guests in this location were also taking the Disney Bus Transportation and returning from the parks. Just because they had been here for two, three, or four days did not mean they were less deserving of a welcome. For them, we shared a "welcome back" or "how was your day?" or some other greeting to let them know that we appreciated them and their business.

On some days, there could be hundreds of thousands of guests on the property at the Walt Disney World Resort. Every one of them expects to be treated like a VIP, and Disney knows that expectation needs to be met. The simplest way to do it is to train, retrain, and reinforce to the Cast that **greeting every guest** is the easiest way to make them feel special. Guests who feel special are more likely to return. Guests who return spend more money. Money to the company means you have a job, and a raise, and so on.

I know...It's a very simple model that Disney leaders are encouraged to reinforce with their teams over, and over, and over. Conversely, if you think of your co-workers as your "internal customers," you can create a great place to work. It's important for you to get out of your office or cubicle and walk your areas to talk to your co-workers and team members.

How can greetings create a culture in your organization where every guest feels special?

## Action Items

- Train your brain to remind yourself that your customer has chosen your organization over others, and a simple "hello" or "welcome back" could turn a one-time customer into a lifelong customer.

- Look for easy "apparel signs" to personalize the greeting. Customers who wear "signage" as apparel usually enjoyed being recognized and talking about it.
    - Family reunions (25th annual Jones Family reunion)
    - Sports Teams (college, NFL, NBA, etc.)
    - Grandparents shirts ("Ask me about my grandkids!")
    - Company Logos (Fred's Tire and Auto, Marriott proud, etc.)
    - Cities or States (Yellowstone Park, NYC, Gulf Shores, etc.)

- Never assume that another employee has greeted or spoken with a customer. Assume that you may be the first contact they have had with anyone at your company.

# 31.

## Approach and be Approachable to all Guests

Disney trains and encourages its Cast Members to be on the lookout for the following guests:

- Those standing on Main Street USA looking at a map and holding it upside down.
- Those in Epcot looking around for the Tree of Life (which is in the Animal Kingdom).
- Those who are stopped and staring at a wall, a shop, or the sky.
- Those who are arguing about the correct location of Peter Pan's Flight ("It's THIS way...No, it's this way!")

Disney trains its employees to look for the guests who look confused. Rather than wait for them to come to you, you go to them. I see this a lot in my local grocery stores. If there are no customers in line, then the cashiers will be standing at the endcap of their aisle. This allows them to be visible to the customers who may have a quick question, and allows them to look for customers (like me) who may be wandering aimlessly looking for the nutmeg on aisle seven when it is OBVIOUSLY kept on aisle two! Who knew?

The other obvious benefit of seeking out guest contact is that it becomes another area of immediate feedback for your organization. By approaching guests and asking them questions, you soon find out the following...

- We need more signage in this area.
- We did not communicate this sale very well.
- We should have used social media in a different way.

Most guests I approached at Disney did not want to complain. They just needed some information or help. Those that did not need help were just happy that someone asked. Disney trains its Cast Members different ways to 'read the guest' to know when a guest needs assistance, and when they want to be left alone.

## Action Items

- *Look for those customers that look lost, confused, or discombobulated.*

- *Be well versed in all areas of your company so that you can answer as many questions as you can, or at least refer the customer in the right direction.*

- *Look for easy talking points with your customers by viewing their apparel, or just listening for keywords or concepts when they talk.*

# 32.

# Offer Service Recovery Quickly

One day, a guest at Disney's Port Orleans Resort returned to the front desk within one hour of receiving his room key. There was a slight problem with his room when he walked into it. He wanted to let me know about it, and he also asked to be compensated for his trouble.

I informed him that I would call our housekeeping staff right away and have them attend to his issue. He appreciated my efforts and reminded me that he would like to be compensated.

I let him know that not only would I send housekeeping up to his room right away, but that I would have a housekeeping manager personally check his room every day at 3:00 pm to assure him that it was cleaned to both his and our expectations.

He said that would be great...and he still asked for compensation for his issue.

The moral of the story is simple. When possible, always try to correct mistakes by providing unparalleled service BEFORE you decide if you have to offer some type of compensation.

Disney makes mistakes every day. It's impossible not to make mistakes. But the key is to admit the mistakes and then try to fix them with service first (a phone call, a personal visit, an apology). If nothing else works, then you may have to take alternate action if you decide you want to keep this customer.

When you make a decision that backfires, all you have to do is get with the customer and say

- "We're sorry."
- "We dropped the ball."
- "We gave you the wrong information. We made a mistake, we own it, and we are sorry."

That's the best type of recovery you can give to your guests. Let them know that you're human, and always try to fix any issue with service first.

## Action Items

- *Ask your manager/owner to share how much money your company spends/refunds/discounts every year based on poor customer service.*

- *Create training programs, videos, or modules that explain the concept of service recovery and the value it adds to your bottom line.*

- *Measure what departments or areas get the most customer complaints and enhance your management and training in those areas to minimize those issues.*

# 33.

## Exhibit Appropriate Body Language

Disney trains its Cast Members to display appropriate body language at all times. This means when you're onstage in a theme park, or a resort, or anywhere on Disney property, you have to give a positive impression with your body language. That means there is no...

- leaning
- looking down
- crossing of the arms
- eye-rolling or "looks"
- crazy facial expressions
- eating onstage or smoking onstage

While this may sound extreme, you have to take into consideration the original vision that Walt Disney had for Disneyland. Walt spent time taking his daughters to amusement parks and carnivals where all the ride operators and food/beverage people looked dirty, unfriendly, and unsafe. In fact, Walt's wife, Lillian, asked him why he would want to build an amusement park since they were all so dirty.

Walt responded, "That's just the point. Mine wouldn't be."

And that is why body language is so important. If you look disinterested while working at Space Mountain, how do I know you are taking my safety seriously? If you are leaning back with your arms crossed in Pecos Bill's Café, how do I know you really want to take my order (and my money)?

The body language of your employees can make or break the customer experience. Walt Disney thought so, and you should as well.

## Action Items

- Do some secret shopping of your employees when they are out on the floor. Do they have the body language that is appropriate for your organization?

- Have your leadership team add "positive body language" to a list of the non-negotiable traits of all employees in your organization.

- Make a list of all types of positive and negative body language and add those to your employee training or departmental meetings. Share the value of a lifelong customer and how body language plays an important role.

# 34.

# Keep Backstage Stuff Backstage

Disney is all about preserving the magic for its guests, and rightfully so. Their main product is magic.

That means the guests don't want to see Snow White and Cinderella on their smoke breaks. That means the guests really don't want to know that the person in that Goofy costume is a person at all. That means the guests don't want to know if and when employees are having a bad day.

This makes perfect sense when you are selling magic.

But what does it mean to you when your product is not "magic"? What if you work in health care, manufacturing, the financial industry, automotive, a small business, or any other type of company?

It means you need to apply the same logic. Your customers do not want to know, and frankly do not care, about the same types of things. The old saying, "no one wants to see how the sausage is made" is very true. So, here are some things for you to think about. Your guests...

- do not want to overhear your employees talking about why they did not get their break on time.
- do not want to see piles and piles of returned items, boxes of supplies, or messy areas in your stores.
- do not care that the person they came to see has to reschedule because they are home with a hangover.
- do not want to see a server or cook coming out of a bathroom stall and not washing their hands before they head back to work.

Your guests want the same thing from you that they want from a visit to a Disney theme park. They want the appearance (read: magic) that every process is going off without a hitch....and when bad things happen, they don't want to hear, "this happens all the time."

Putting Disney Magic in your organization means never letting them see how your sausage is made!

## Action Items

- *Create an environment of "onstage" behaviors and "backstage" behaviors with your employees, and share/train the expected behaviors of each.*

- *Ask your employees in a team meeting what the phrase "no one wants to see how the sausage is made" means to them. Ask them to share things that they do not want to see when they are a customer. Then ask them to translate those into their current teams and roles.*

- *Make sure that your guest-facing areas are always "show-ready" and that they don't resemble a large storage closet.*

# 35.

# Thank Every Guest Every Time

*"Thank you!"*

*"Thanks for coming today!"*

*"Thank you for choosing to spend your limited disposable income with our company instead of another one. I really need this job, and your money helps pay my electricity, mortgage, grocery bill, and gas bill. You are also helping to fund my kid's college education as well as my 401(k). Without your business today, I am not even sure what I would do. So, from the bottom of my heart, I thank you."*

While the last one is extreme, the truth is, those thoughts should be present with every employee during every guest interaction.

I firmly believe that without customers, you have no business being in business. Disney believes that every guest is important, that no guest should be overlooked, and that each and every guest should be thanked for every transaction.

Here is another example. Chick-Fil-A (CFA) prides itself on training its employees to say "My pleasure" after a guest thanks them.

Guest: *"Thank you."*

CFA employee: *"It's my pleasure."*

While the premise is correct as it reinforces their value of wanting to provide excellent service, the reality is that all organizations should follow something like this:

Guest: *"Thank you."*

Employee: *"No. Thank YOU for coming in today. We truly appreciate you."*

A customer who comes into your business, chooses you over the competition, and spends ANY amount of money in your company deserves your thanks. Make sure your employees know the value of a sincere "thank you!"

### Action Items

- *Remind each and every employee that a powerful thank-you, when sincere, will most often create a return guest, which could turn them into a lifelong guest!*

- *Include the power of a "Thank-You" in all your training sessions.*

- *Form a cross-functional team to come up with a standard thank-you response that all employees will use to ensure consistency and promote your brand.*

# 36.

## Be a Guest in your own Organization

Disney encourages its Cast Members to be a guest in their own organization.

This is why Cast Members and their families are given park passes to attend the parks on their days off. Yes, it is a benefit, and yes, it is designed to be fun. But it serves a third purpose as well. It allows the Cast Member to walk a mile in the guests' shoes so that they are better equipped to handle customer interactions and situations.

As a leader, you should try and do business with your own company as a guest. When's the last time you've looked at your company's website? When's the last time you've tried to use the 'contact us' button on that website? When's the last time you filled out the questionnaire form on your website to see how long it takes for someone to get back with you? When's the last time you've called your toll-free number (or any phone number) and see how long it takes for any employee to answer? When is the last time you visited one of your locations as a customer so you could see how you were treated? (This assumes that no one would recognize you).

This is something you need to do no matter what role you play in your company. Whether you are a CEO, CFO, middle management, front line management, or employee at any level – being a leader means you must get out there and experience your own product.

If you don't experience your organization as a guest, you will be unable to empathize with your guests when they share some constructive feedback with you. You will assume they are wrong, crazy, or just got a bad employee on a bad day. On the other hand, if you actually experience what they experience, you are more likely to fix it or improve upon it.

Make some time to be a customer in your own company.

### Action Items

- *Make sure all employees at all levels know that it is an expectation that they become a customer at least twice per year in their own organization.*

- *If you are in the service industry, the employees should experience the service. If you are in manufacturing, the employees should do a random phone call to ask a couple of questions about your products*

- *Remember, the goal is not to catch the employees doing something wrong. The goal is to experience the same thing that your customers experience, as this will help you act upon and fix/improve your levels of service.*

## 37.

# Create a Sense of Anticipation

Sometimes getting there is half the fun. A road trip to the Walt Disney World Resort is filled with anticipation. It comes from the excitement of driving on the roads, seeing the billboards, and hearing the welcome music on the Disney radio station blare through your vehicle. Today, Disney takes it to a whole different level.

- They send out magic bands ahead of time.
- They'll send you magazines and marketing reminders.
- They'll send you downloadable items, such as a countdown clock that counts the days until your next Disney vacation.

They work to create an absolute sense of anticipation of going to visit a Disney theme park or going to see a Disney movie.

Let's talk about your organization and customers.

- Do your customers have a sense of anticipation when they visit?
- If it's a restaurant, are they excited about new menu items you've been communicating in advance?
- If it's a health care organization, have you been sending them information about new doctors and the new, efficient check-in process?
- If it's an an oil-change location, have you sent them information about the great things that are going to happen once they arrive and all the extra services you provide after they arrive?

It does not matter if you are in health care, finance, or some other non-traditional customer-service-focused business. People want to anticipate a visit to you. Maybe the anticipation is the fact that they want to see the people that are nice that work there. Creating anticipation needs to be intentional, not an afterthought. Anticipation is a significant part of the entire customer experience.

## Action Items

- Do your guests anticipate coming to your location? What can you do to create a sense of anticipation? Get a few people together in your organization and talk about how you can create a sense of anticipation.

- Look for different ways to communicate that anticipation. Does it need to be a phone call, an e-mail, something on social media, or a mailer? There are multiple ways to share some anticipatory information.

- Make sure that the experience lives up to the anticipation that you are selling.

# 38.

# Deliver an Amazing Welcome

On the first day of new-hire orientation, Walt Disney World Cast Members are told that everyone is responsible for welcoming our guests. It is not just the job of the toll plaza hostess. It is not just the job of the tram driver. It is not just the job of the person taking the ticket. It is not the job of the person in the restaurant. When the guest arrives, it is everyone's responsibility to say welcome.

And why is that?

It's because the welcome sets the tone for the entire day. The welcome lets people know that you appreciate them. Customers have a choice in just about every area of business these days, and if they don't feel welcome at your organization, they will choose to go somewhere else.

A simple greeting, some eye contact. "We're glad you're here."

These things tie in perfectly to create a sense of welcome for your guests. What are you doing to create the perfect welcome?

## Action Items

- *Look around at how you welcome your guests. Is there signage? Are your employees trained properly? Does every employee know it's their responsibility to welcome somebody to your place of business, even if it's in the parking lot or in an offstage area?*

- *Train and develop your employees to know the power of "the welcome." Sometimes people need to remember that the welcome plays a huge part in the overall experience.*

- *Create consistent and meaningful welcomes when possible. Perhaps you have a signature phrase, a slogan, a song, or something else to welcome the guests. It is important that the first impression is not just the welcome, but the overall first impression of the organization that may include sight, sound, smell, taste, and touch.*

# 39.

# Produce a Powerful, Unforgettable Experience

The experience is everything; the experience is second to none. The experience includes the moment your guests arrive on your property to the moment they leave. What are they experiencing?

How is the customer service experience at Disney? The experience includes things that are above what you might expect...

- It's the sights, smells, taste, and touch of a theme park.
- It's the shows.
- It's the parade.
- It's the Cast Members.
- It's the trash that may or may not be on the ground.
- It's the paint that may or may not be chipping.
- It's the way that one Cast Member treats them versus another Cast member.
- It's the guest connecting the dots with what they thought should happen and what actually happens.
- It's when things go wrong. How are they corrected?
- It's the body language of the employees.

- It's the way that the guest feels at the beginning, middle, and end of their visit.

These items are all part of the overall experience. And they may be the most important part of the guest experience. If the experience falls flat...If the food is cold...If the people are rude, then none of the other steps matter (anticipation, welcome, etc.). Make sure that you have everything in place to provide an awesome customer experience to every customer, each and every time.

## Action Items

- *What are the different levels of experience that customers receive? Is there a VIP experience versus another type of experience? Think how you feel when you are called last to board an airplane because you are not a platinum level guest. How important is it to you that each and every customer receive the same level of service?*

- *If you do have experiences above and beyond, such as Disney's FastPass or priority dining, does every customer have access to these? Do you make all of these perks available and understandable so that if some customers are getting a different experience than others, they at least know why?*

- *Make sure that you consider the "Disney Show" element when thinking about your business. It plays a huge part in the guest experience.*

# 40.

## Provide a Proper Guest Farewell

The farewell can make or break the guest experience.

Think about it. If guests at Disney are having a fantastic experience, **and** if their kids were well-behaved all day, **and** all the attractions were open, **and** they had very short lines, **and** the food was good, then they will be in a pleasant mood when they leave the park. **Then, to top it all off, employees tell them** "Thank you for coming." "We appreciate you." "Thanks so much." "We can't wait to see you again." That just validates that they have made the right decision, and it encourages them to return.

The opposite is true as well.

If the customer had a bad experience, and it was crowded, and their kids were angry, and there was lots of yelling, a Cast Member placed at the exit saying, "Thank you for coming, we hope you had a good time" can serve two purposes.

1. It may possibly be the one shining light to a bad day where they say, "Well, at least they're thanking me for coming, even though this day was a mess."

2. It could provide one last chance for service recovery as guests may tell the employees that they had a bad time because of a bad experience. In turn, the employee can then apologize, solve and make it right, and maybe even stay in contact with them in one way or the other.

In any event, don't discount the power of the farewell. Having people at the end of your event saying, "Goodbye!" or "Thank you, we know you could have gone anywhere, but you chose to come here!" makes a powerful impression on customers these days who think they're always being treated as a number.

### Action Items

- Do you have a farewell process in place at your business for when people leave? Does everybody know to say thank you for coming or goodbye? Are they given a special mint or a reminder to come back? Are they told how much you appreciate their business?

- Look at your organization and decide the correct touchpoints for a proper farewell. What does a farewell look like in different departments?

- Make sure all your employees know that creating a farewell is everyone's role. Even if you're walking in from the parking lot and see a guest leaving and you didn't wait on them, it's still every employee's responsibility to say, "Thank you for coming," even if they were already told that multiple times before they left.

# 41.

## Allow Guests to Savor the Experience

What does it mean to savor something?

To savor is to appreciate – to relish – to fondly remember.

Do all of your customers feel that your version of Disney magic provided them with memories to savor?

Yes, they were anticipating a great experience. You gave them a good welcome. They had a good experience, and you said goodbye.

But what if a Disney guest is not thinking about what a great time they had upon their return home? Disney wants its guests to tell others what a great time they had. Disney wants them planning their next expedition to a Disney theme park or resort. If the guest is not doing this via "savoring," then all that hard work in the prior four steps is for naught (anticipate, welcome, experience, farewell).

The same thing holds true in your organization. When people leave your restaurant, your doctor's office, your school, or your place of business and they had a great experience, are any of the following things happening?

- Are they telling their friends about it?
- Are they thinking that it was well worth the price?
- Are they already planning their next trip?

That's the power of savoring. It is an important part of your overall guest experience cycle to make sure that guests (and employees) know that the customer experience does not end when they leave your property.

The customer experience continues back at home over dinner tables telling others about the experience they had with your organization. That leads to more lifelong customers and more new guests. That's the power of savoring.

## Action Items

- *What do you do to encourage savoring? Do you send out surveys? Do you send out follow-up emails or make phone calls to remind people how much you appreciated them?*

- *If you don't have a savoring process in place, can you create one?*

- *How can you use social media sites like Facebook, LinkedIn, Twitter, and Instagram to allow customers to savor what they experienced and spark a desire to come back again and again?*

## 42.

# Generate a Consistent Guest Experience

Consistency is the simplest way to add magic to the guests. It is also one of the most difficult things for Disney to do

And it's also one of the things they do exceptionally well.

Think about it.

Despite the over thirty thousand acres, forty-three square miles, four theme parks, over 24 hotels, and a shopping and dining entertainment area, guests continue to expect to be treated exactly the same every single time. That's the power of consistency.

The easiest way to do this is to create non-negotiable customer service standards that stand the test of time. You must ensure that all of your employees learn about these standards on their first day of employment during orientation. The Walt Disney World Resort calls its service standards "The Seven Guest Service Guidelines."

- Greet and welcome each and every guest
- Make eye contact and smile
- Seek out guest contact
- Provide immediate service recovery
- Display appropriate body language at all times
- Preserve the magical guest experience
- Thank each and every guest

By utilizing these service guidelines and training them on day one, every Cast Member knows they are expected to demonstrate these standards. This is true for every Cast Member - no matter if they work in parks, resorts, water parks, front of the house, or back of the house. They know what is expected of them. This is the magic of a consistent guest experience.

## Action Items

- *Do you have non-negotiable customer service standards? If yes, are they shared on the employee's first day? If not, why not?*

- *If you don't have customer service standards in place, create them. However, don't create them at the executive level. Create a focus group that includes front-line employees.*

- *Train your managers to hold employees accountable, and to give consistent customer service using the guidelines that you developed. This doesn't mean they can't go off-script to be creative and innovative every now and then, but the basic foundational principles of the non-negotiable standards must be followed at all times to prevent inconsistent application and inconsistent guest experiences.*

# 43.

# Create Emotional and Relational Connections

Creating an emotional connection with your customers is something that very few organizations consider necessary.

Disney does this well, and it's something you can be involved with in your company.

What are some ways you can create emotional connections or relational connections with your customers?

First, you have to realize is that no matter how much technology you have and how much state-of-the-art infrastructure you have, the core being of most humans desire a connection or relationship with another person. This is why we are constantly touching zero on our phones to "speak to an operator." We want to talk to a real, live human being.

Disney likes to connect with people through the power of pins, buttons, stickers, and personal relationships. We want each guest to think that they are the most important guest in the world...because they are! We don't want them to feel like just a number. Disney doesn't want them to feel like they are just being pushed through a theme park. We want them to feel like they're enjoying the most magical experience that they can with personalized service, even though they are surrounded by tens of thousands of other people.

One example of this is when Disney changed a job title from "custodial host" to "custodial guest services." They realized that the frontline custodial hosts were having the most interactions with the guests. It was important that they have the skill set to build relationships with each guest. Disney wants the custodial guest services team to provide custodial services, but also to talk with the guests, connect with the guests, and make relationships with the guests. What can you do in your organization to help other frontline employees build those incredible connections with the customers?

## Action Items

- *How are you creating emotional or relational connections with your customers? Make a list of all the ways in which you think you are currently doing this in your organization.*

- *Think of a way that you can set yourself apart and differentiate yourself from your competitors by creating relationships. Should you call people instead of emailing them? Should all small children get a sticker when they arrive at your place of business? What can you do?*

- *Once you have a successful way to build relationships, don't save it for just one department. Make sure it is shared across the organization so others can employ the idea as well.*

# 44.

# Add Creativity to your Customer Service

It's no longer enough to just give average customer service. In fact, it's not enough to give above average or excellent customer service. We've come to a point in customer interactions where you need to add creativity to your excellent customer service in order to gain new customers and retain the current customers.

So how does Disney do it? How does Disney provide more creative customer service than their competitors?

First of all, they don't minimize any idea from anyone when it comes to customer service, as even the simplest ideas may be more creative than others. Walt once remarked that he would take a creative idea from any level of employee...especially if it was a good idea. Some creative things to do in the hospitality industry would include...

- stopping and singing in the middle of a check-in process.
- delivering a personalized knock on the door from the person who checked them into their hotel room to ask them how their stay is going.
- a handwritten note on the guest receipt that tells them how much they appreciate them.

Disney constantly asks themselves, "What can we do that no one else is doing in our industry?" That's where creativity kicks in. And this is something you can do in your organization.

Yes, you should always strive to give excellent customer service, but creativity is the fun part!

### Action Items

- *Inspire your employees to be creative. Ask them what they would do to build fun, creative customer service interactions? Then document all their ideas and make a master list to research and act upon. Look into what your competition is doing.*

- *See what the industry trends are and then try and improve upon them.*

- *Never discount any idea from any employee. Sometimes the best ideas come from the least likely of places.*

## Section Four

# The Magic of Business Processes

*Do you want your company to be the best?*
*Do you have a passion for creating a successful organization?*

*This chapter is designed for the CEO, management,*
*and leadership teams, but there are plenty of Disney tips here*
*that anyone at any level could add to their workplace.*

# 45.

# Share the Heritage and Traditions of your Organization

Sharing and modeling the heritage and traditions of your company cannot be overstated. It is the backbone of what makes the Disney organization run. Every single employee who works for The Walt Disney Company learns about the heritage and traditions of the company.

They learn about Walt Disney and his family. They learn about the history of the organization. They learn about animation, theme parks, film, and television. They learn about the mistakes Disney made and the opportunities that Disney has.

Are you doing the same at your company?

Sometimes people will push back and say, "We don't have any heritage in our company. We had one person start the company back in the day and no one knows a thing about them." Well, that's not going to help you be successful. If you truly want people to be devoted to your organization, they should know the history behind it. Here are some things to think about:

- When was your company started?
- Who were the founders of your company?
- What are some trials and tribulations they overcame?
- Did you ever go through a buyout or a merger?
- When was the first female or minority leader of your department hired, and how can you showcase that?
- Where does the company stand today versus where it stood years ago?
- Is there a quote from your original founder or owner that you can share?

When you talk about the history and traditions of your organization, people will feel committed to it. It's very easy with The Walt Disney Company because of the immense amount of history and tradition, but it can be applied to any organization. People want to know why the company they work for or patronize exists, who created it, and why they should be proud to work or visit there. People want to feel like they are part of something bigger.

Don't just **share** the heritage and traditions of your company, but **model** them every day. Talk about how great the company is, where it comes from, the great things the future holds. In fact, the Walt Disney Company (through the Disney University) rolls out regular training about Walt Disney and his history because people love to learn. It reinforces a connection with them. Perhaps you can create a similar training class for your organization.

## Action Items

- Do some research on the history and traditions of your company. Find out everything you can.

- Document and create infographics or training classes about the history and traditions of your organization.

- Make sure that you are doing everything you can within your power to share the importance and passion of your company's heritage and traditions. Let people understand the value behind it.

# 46.

# Use Leadership Development for Succession Planning

Succession planning is of the utmost importance in any organization. Companies that don't have a promotional pipeline are destined to fail. The Walt Disney Company realizes the importance of succession planning and creates management development programs internally that will help prepare Cast Members for their next roles.

Ron Holyfield, an author and expert in servant leadership, once told me that it is so important to "Practice before you promote." Why wait until someone gets promoted to train them and develop them? Instead, train them in advance so they are ready to move to their next job.

When I worked at Disney there were multiple iterations of a leadership development program. It began as the Disney Management Development Program...which morphed into the Disney Leadership Development Program...which then morphed into Crossroads to Leadership...and so on, and so on. The changes happened because you must update or you will perish. Periodically, the organization must revisit the content, research new theories and trends in leadership development, and update the program as necessary. Every successful organization needs a management and leadership development training program in-house for the high performers.

Employees at Disney went through a rigorous interview process and were hand-selected to go through these programs. They were trained and coached and put into temporary management roles. Now not every organization can do this. In fact, working in local government, I understand the struggles of leadership development and succession planning. It's hard to handpick somebody for the next role and not be accused of breaking some type of law, rule, regulation, or policy. But it can be done. And in the private sector, it has to be done.

There is no reason in today's world of aging baby boomers and plentiful young talent that we cannot have some type of training and succession plan in place for our high performers. It is imperative for the future of your organization.

## Action Items

- What type of internal management preparation, leadership development, or training is available for your employees? Make sure you know what that is and that you share the information with your team.

- What type of succession plan is in place for your employees? Make sure that it is documented and advertised so people know that it is transparent.

- If nothing is available in your organization, can you create something in your department? If the organization decides not to focus on succession planning and management development, at least do something in your team. Look at your direct reports and decide how you're going to motivate, inspire, train, and develop them to be ready for the next level.

# 47.

# Live your Vision / Mission / Values every day

It is difficult to memorize your corporate vision, mission, and values when they are long and convoluted. It's hard to be passionate about them when you don't remember them. If they are just words on a bulletin board or a couple of notes on the back of an I.D. card, no one will get behind them, support them, and live them.

Disney strives to make sure that its mission, vision, and values are lived, breathed, talked about, and incorporated into the everyday aspect of the work. While there are many different corporate ways to explain vision and mission, Disney always believed that vision was "what you wanted your organization to be", while the mission was "how you were going to achieve it". Underlying both vision and mission are your company values.

The Disney values are typically presented as an acronym: ORCHID B! Openness, Respect, Courage, Honesty, Integrity, Diversity, and Balance. These values were talked about in team meetings. They were talked about during the onboarding process. There was always a discussion to make sure that your personal values aligned with the corporate values. This was important to corporate success, as there were some Disney Cast members who felt like their personal values may not align with corporate values. For example, one might say "I am not comfortable with honesty as I think some things are better left unsaid." Disney would share that even though you may not agree with these values, it is important for each person to display the values and behaviors that the organization expects of you and is ultimately paying you to display. If you cannot do that, you will not be successful in the Disney organization.

When I arrived at local government, I tried to add this to our department. We did not have any stated values for our department. After careful consideration and team discussions, we came up with our departmental values. The four we agreed upon form an acronym – FLAG – Flexible, Lively, Approachable, and Genuine. We try to live by these values every day.

People may say it's silly to make acronyms, but it's so much easier for people to memorize and live your values when it's a word that they can remember. Look at your values. Apply them every day. Then encourage people to live them.

## Action Items

- Find out the core values of your organization. If there are none, create them.

- Always have your values fall into an acronym. If your current values don't make an acronym, make one so that people can remember them easier.

- Talk about your values in staff meetings, department head meetings, and all team meetings. The more you talk about them, the more you remember them, and the more people will apply them on a daily basis.

# 48.

## Research your Competition

When I worked at the Walt Disney World Resort, we would always talk about our competitor (Universal Studios) which is right down the I-4 corridor. In fact, there was a "theme park war" around 1989 between Walt Disney World and Universal Studios to see who could open their movie-based theme park first. Walt Disney World won, and Disney-MGM Studios opened almost a year ahead of Universal Studios. I'll never forget throughout the 1990s when I would hear our executive leadership team say, "Universal Studios is not our competition. Our competition is Las Vegas, and the Bahamas, and the beaches, and anywhere people go on vacation. Period."

While that may be somewhat true, the reality was that Universal Studios, Sea World, and Busch Gardens were our main competitors in Central Florida.

So what can you do? You need to know what's going on in other organizations.

Great leaders should never put our head in the sand and say, "I don't care what the restaurant down the street is doing," or "I don't care what the school system down the street is doing," or "I don't care what the health care system across town is doing."

Yes, you do. And yes, you should.

There is nothing wrong with checking on your competitors. You never want to lie, cheat, steal, or use other's information for your own gain. However, there is nothing illegal or unethical with having a greater understanding of all companies that are in competition with you.

Always keep your eyes and ears open for what your competition is doing. Disney does and it always helps them become better. You want to be creative and innovative in your own way, but always be aware of what your competition is doing so they don't beat you at your own game.

## Action Items

- *Who are your main competitors within five miles? Twenty miles? Fifty miles?*

- *Do research on your competition. Use the internet, secret shoppers, annual reports, industry trade publications, and on-site visits to know what your competition is doing.*

- *Find the best practices that your competitors are doing and improve on them. Enhance them and find ways to make them even better.*

## 49.

## Always put Company over Department

It is an overused cliché to "work smarter, not harder," but it is an essential part of the Disney organization, and it is a secret to their success. The Disney quality standards for the theme parks and resorts division are safety, courtesy, show, and efficiency. Efficiency is nothing more than working smarter and not harder, and the main focus of that is partnering with other organizations within the company.

I know many people who work for a company where the individual departments live in silos and put their own needs over those of the organization. I have worked with many companies like these, where it is hard to get people working from the same script.

At the Walt Disney World Resort, we tried very hard not to do that. Sure, there was always some slight competition between the Magic Kingdom, Epcot, Disney-MGM Studios (now Disney's Hollywood Studios) and the Animal Kingdom. Disney's Port Orleans Resort wants to have higher guest satisfaction ratings than Disney's Yacht Club Resort or Disney's All-Star Sports Resort. There is inherent competition in all of us. However, the overall growth of the company is of higher importance than the individual resort or park.

In order to work smarter and not harder, it is important to share resources. Disney would cross-utilize Cast Members during tough times. The resort general managers would frequently meet and share if their guest ratings went up or down. Disney resorts would often pilot a new program at one resort and then try it at another, and then roll it out among all of them.

When you work smarter and not harder, you put the needs of the company over the needs of the individual departments. That's how you drive a successful organization.

## Action Items

- Take a look at your corporate culture and decide if you can work smarter and not harder, or are the silos too deep and too entrenched for you to work together?

- Create a board of directors with managers from each department who can share best practices, what's working, and how you can share resources during times of need.

- Put together a financial spreadsheet that shows how the benefits of working together outweigh the cost of everybody working independently. Why have three departments offering the same thing? If you combine your resources, you can have one department offering something even greater for both the guests and the customers.

# 50.

# Showcase your Organization in New and Unusual Ways

The Walt Disney Company is a self-promoting marketing machine. Just a few of the ways they self-promote include:

- Holiday parade specials on TV
- Behind-the-Scenes tours in the theme parks
- Company-sponsored blogs and podcasts
- Internal TV station at all resorts
- YouTube videos
- Former Cast Members sharing good things.

That last one is very important to me. There are many former Disney Cast Members (like myself) who speak, train, and share the magic of Disney with other companies.

Now, I realize that your company cannot put a parade on ABC each year. But there are multiple other ways that you can self-promote that could help your bottom line.

- Can you sponsor a local parade, a humanitarian effort, a local sports team, a local road for cleanup purposes, etc.?
- Can you secure a weekly one-on-one talk with a local radio or TV show that showcases your company in a way you want?
- Can your CEO put out weekly YouTube videos where he/she showcases a customer of the month?

The only bad idea is those that are not brought up. The only bad ideas are those that are not shared in the conference room or at the brainstorming session.

Make sure you think of new, exciting, and innovative ways for both employees and customers to showcase the value of your organization in new and exciting ways.

### Action Items

- *Take a look at your current marketing/PR strategies. How many are true and tested, and how many are new, different, exciting, and untested? Create a balance to offer both.*

- *Find your most loyal/frequent customers and ask them for reasons they keep coming back. Then ask them for the craziest way to share that. See if you can implement their idea and give them credit for it.*

- *Remind yourself that this is not about web clicks, ROI, or revenue numbers. Showcasing your company may cost a little bit of money, but it also keeps your company's name on the lips of all consumers.*

# 51.

# Embrace the Concept of "Synergy"

Synergy is a simple business staple that is lived throughout every line of business in The Walt Disney Company (TWDC). The first real example of this happened with the release of the animated feature "The Lion King" in 1994. In addition to the movie, the company realized that it would benefit from synergizing The Lion King by...

- Creating a Live-Action Puppet Show at the Magic Kingdom (which eventually led to a spectacular live-action show at Disney's Animal Kingdom Theme Park)
- Filling up The Disney Stores with lots of merchandise
- Creating a Broadway Show at the Disney branded Theater on Broadway
- And so on and so on

Years later, when TWDC rolled out its new Disney+ Streaming service, the concept of synergy was alive and well. You heard about Disney+ in multiple ways:

- ABC and ESPN shows were promoting the roll-out date
- Disney Theme parks shrink-wrapped their buses and other transportation modes to announce the new service
- Banners and information on Disney+ were placed in theme parks around the globe

The beauty of synergy is that it allows all areas of your company to work together to showcase another area, and the end result is greater than just one segment could garner working by itself.

Synergy is not just to be used by large corporate behemoths. You and your company can benefit from the power of synergy as well.

### Action Items

- *Can one department help share information or promote an event in another department?*

- *Take a look at success initiatives from department to department or shift to shift. Think of new and creative ways that each side can assist the other.*

- *Start using the concepts of synergy to build successful initiatives.*

# 52.

## Allow for a Culture of Creative Risk-Taking

Disney did not get to be successful by playing it safe. Disney is successful due to a very strategic decision to allow for calculated-risk taking at all levels of the organization.

Disney has had its share of flops, mistakes, and closures. From theme parks to resorts, to television and multi-media, and even to merchandising and digital media...there have been many mistakes made along the way. However, the beauty of failure is that it allows employees to learn, grow, and create something even bigger and better.

But it all starts at the top.

If the CEO does not create a culture of calculated risk-taking, then creativity and innovation will never appear.

If the President does not minimize the fear-factor that exists in many corporate cultures, then the employees will not step outside their comfort zones.

If the leadership team does not allow for mistakes, then new ideas and new initiatives will not bubble up to the top.

If front-line managers do not drive a culture of taking calculated risks, then the organization will be what it has always been, and the customers will get what they always got...and your competition will soon pass you by.

Note: I am not talking about risks that may cost you millions of dollars or lead the company to the verge of bankruptcy. I am asking you to allow your employees to be creative and innovative. I hope you will accept new ideas from all levels of the organization. I want you to be head and shoulders above your competition, and that only comes with a culture that encourages calculated risk-taking.

## Action Items

- *Ask your employees if they think your corporate culture encourages risk-taking.*

- *Is there a culture of fear when it comes to making mistakes? Are your front-line managers documenting small mistakes and encouraging fear, or are they coaching and developing when mistakes are made?*

- *Make a list of the last few projects/decisions/successes that happened due to an employee or department taking a calculated risk? Showcase the good things that can happen when that is allowed.*

# 53.

# Provide Multiple "Purpose Streams" for all Employees

What do I mean when I say "purpose streams?" This goes well beyond mission, vision, and values.

Purpose streams are organization-wide messaging points that allow every employee to track with the underlying reasons that the organization exists. Most companies share their vision, mission, and values, and hope that is enough to drive employee morale and guest loyalty. But Disney takes it well beyond vision, mission, and values.

Lee Cockerell was my Executive Vice President when I worked at Disney, and he did a phenomenal job of collecting all of the different 'purpose' statements that existed and combined them into one document for employees at all levels. It was part of his "The Main Street Diary" employee communication document, and it was titled "Special Edition: Why we do what we do AND how we do what we do." This document contained all of our streams of purpose...including, but not limited to:

- Performance Excellence
- Our Vision
- Disney Heritage and Traditions
- Quality Standards
- Guest Experience Cycle
- Four Cast Expectations
- Our Goal
- Role in the Show
- Eight Cast Service Guidelines for Leaders of Leaders
- Leadership Competencies
- Our Commitment
- Our Disney Culture and our Disney Values
- Disney's Great Leader Strategies
- Disney Traits and Behaviors
- Four Guest Expectations
- Leadership Traits for Performance Excellence
- Our Purpose and Our Role
- Seven Guest Service Guidelines for Guests
- Seven Cast Service Guidelines for Front-Line Leaders
- Statement of Purpose

This document served two main purposes. One, it kept everything in one place. All managers, leaders, and employees knew where to look to hold each other accountable. This was not an official document from HR that had to be signed and upheld. It was a document that shared our streams of purpose in one easy location.

Second, it reminded Cast Members every day that there was always something bigger than them. When you read this document and saw what is expected, you realize what an honor and privilege it is to be part of something bigger than the vision, mission, and values.

### Action Items

- *Collect and document all the different streams of purpose that currently exist in your organization – statements of purpose, values, standards, etc.*

- *Place them all into one document that is authorized by the CEO, VP, or other high-ranking team member.*

- *Have a rollout day where you share this document, celebrate what it means, and reinforce the entire "How and Why" of what you do in your company every day.*

# 54.

............................

# Look for ways to Enhance the Process

Here in the south, Nick Saban, the head football coach for the University of Alabama, is all about living, breathing, and teaching "the process" to all of his players. It's not about winning games or winning championships. It is about following a well-designed, time-tested, and proven process. His players know that if you do that, the wins will come, the accolades will come, and the successes will come.

The same holds true at Disney, and the same holds true for your organization.

It's not about doing it quicker, faster, or cheaper.

It's not about being first to market.

It is about implementing a structured and effective process for getting work done.

Disney taught me the importance of well-defined processes. From daily track-talks in our attractions to morning role calls in our housekeeping departments, these processes are time-tested, but are always being improved.

Disney brings in its industrial engineers to look at the queue lines in the theme parks and resorts. They measure, and measure, and measure, and when they find the best way at that time, they roll with it, share it with other parks and departments, and refine it over and over.

Keep in mind that the most efficient and effective process is never completed. With new employees, new leadership, new customers, and new technology, the best process will always need to be refined and updated.

But successful organizations never implement a process, stand-back, and say "That is the best it is ever going to get." If that were true, Disney Parks would still be selling ticket books with attractions labeled A-E. Instead, great organizations should always be looking to enhance their processes.

## Action Items

- *Find one process in your department or organization that you know needs to be improved based on either employee or customer feedback.*

- *Create a small committee made up of employees from multiple areas to brainstorm a new and more efficient way for that process.*

- *Keep in mind that some new ways may be free, and others may cost a bit. Decide if the short-term costs are worth it based on the long-term benefits, such as cost savings, improved morale, or increased customer loyalty.*

# 55.

# An employee's First Day is their Most Important Day

The final tip for organizational success may be the only one you really need.

***Do everything in your power to make an employee's first day a great day.***

A great way to lose a high performer is to give them an "average" first-day experience. That's right... just average may be enough to lose them over time.

I was fortunate enough to be a part of the Disney Traditions leadership team for many years. Traditions is the world-famous orientation program that ALL Disney employees must attend. These first-day orientation programs had food and beverage hosts sitting at the same tables with VPs of finance. Housekeepers making minimum wage enjoying the same first-day experience as a resort executive who may make six figures. NO ONE is exempt from attending the Disney Traditions program.

The reason is simple. Every employee needs to hear the same message on day one. Everyone needs to know their role and purpose on day one. The magic of Traditions is that it was not filled with forms and signatures and HR policies. Instead, you spend a full first day learning about the Disney Company, its heritage and traditions, your role in the show, and hopefully meeting and networking with Cast Members across the organization who could become partners and friends in the future.

Having a great first-day experience should not fall solely to the HR or Training department. It needs to be a strategic part of your recruitment and retention strategy. There will be plenty of time to sign papers and fill out forms. The first day should be for emotional connections between your organization and your new employees.

### Action Items

- Take a good, long look at your Day One orientation program. Are there ways that it can be plussed up to create more of an emotional impact between employee and company?

- Allow for current employees to be a part of the first day of orientation. Rather than HR or a company trainer, allow high performing employees who love their jobs to come speak, or perhaps facilitate a part of the day to create connections with new hires.

- Spend whatever money is necessary to make this day a priority as part of your budget.

- Take accurate measurements after the orientation and one year later. What do they remember, and did that day impact how they felt about the company?

Made in the USA
Columbia, SC
07 April 2025